AF291385

First published in India by HarperCollins *Publishers* 2025
HarperCollins *Publishers* India, Cyber City, Building 10-A, Gurugram,
Haryana-122002, India
www.harpercollins.co.in

2 4 6 8 10 9 7 5 3 1



P-ISBN: 9789369897940
E-ISBN: 9789369891146



Cover design: **Shamika Chaves**
Ruskin Bond's photos: **Siddharth Bond**

Typeset in Crimson Pro, Regular, 15 by **Shamika Chaves**

Printed and bound at Thomson Press India Ltd

*

HarperCollins Publishers, Macken House, 39/40 Mayor Street Upper,
Dublin 1, D01 C9W8, Ireland

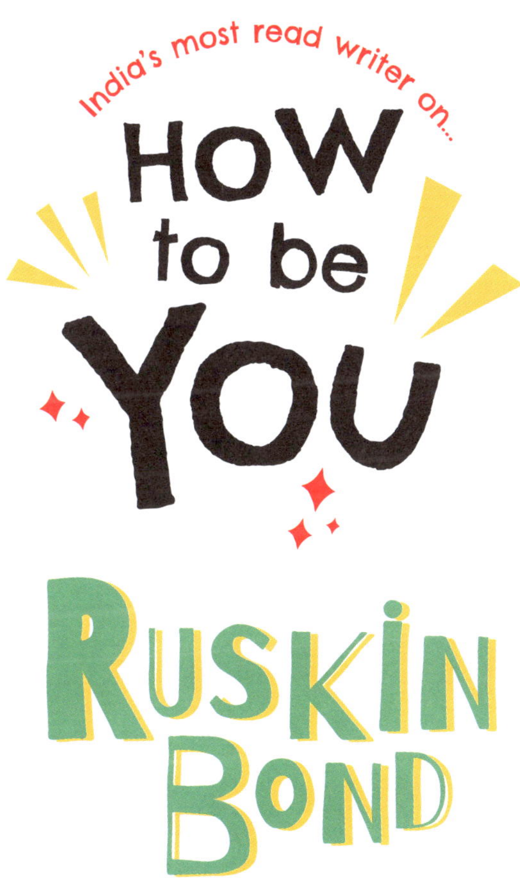


Illustrated & Designed by

Shamika Chaves

HarperCollins *Publishers* India

Speed Post                                    DATE ________

desk of

<u>That Determined Chin!</u>

Dear Reader,
            When I was eighteen,
struggling to get my stories published in
magazines, my manuscripts kept coming back to
me with polite rejection slips. My cousins thought
it a great joke, crazy Ruskin imagining he was a
writer! But an old lady who was present on one
of these occasions said: "Don't give up, son.
You have a determined chin. You'll succeed
one day."
            A determined chin? I looked in the
mirror. My chin was no different from thousands
of other chins. Determination, I was to discover,
existed in the mind and not in the chin — or
the nose or the toes.
            Determination. That was the secret.
And I had plenty of it. The years rolled by, and
I followed my destiny. Boys and girls, adult
men and women, must take the same steep road
to whatever they want to achieve, whether its
fame and fortune or, as in my case, just
a cottage in the hills.
            Keep right on to the end of

Neelgagan

the road. If the road be long, let your heart and mind be strong, and you'll be what you want to be.

Build castles in the air, if you like. But put foundations under them.

Ruskin Bond

From: R. Bond
Ivy Cottage,
Landour Cantt
Mussoorie 248179

# Contents

# How I Became What I Wanted To Become

As a boy,
I took to
books as a
bear takes
to honey!

At school, the library was my favourite place. At home (seldom in one house) I had my tin trunk full of the books I liked and collected.

I WAS IN LOVE WITH THE PRINTED WORD.

And by the time I was sixteen and finished with school, I wanted to make my living from the printed word.

My mother wanted me to be a teacher; my stepfather wanted me to get into the Army.

I was having none of it.

I was determined to be a writer. It was the thing I did best. And shouldn't our lives be directed towards doing what we do best?

Many of my early efforts came back with the "editor's regrets". But I persisted. All those essays and literary prizes I'd won at school had to mean something. And after several attempts I sold a story to a national magazine. I was paid fifty rupees for it. Not bad in 1951! And I made it a rule that I would always insist on being paid for my work.

I was a professional from the beginning. And I'm still one.

I don't believe in paying to be published. It's the author who must be paid – if he's any good.

When I was seventeen, I sailed for England, and there, between jobs, I worked on my first novel. It was called *The Room on the Roof*. As I did not have any money of my own, I had to take up a job. In my three years in the U.K. I worked at different periods, for a travel agency, a grocery store, a photograph agency and the public health department.

I did my
writing at
night or on
holidays.
But before I
was twenty...

I'd found a publisher for my novel.

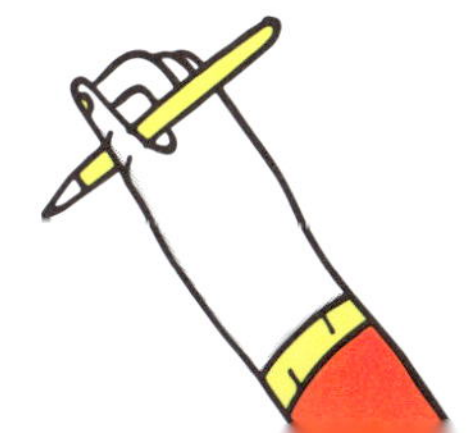

An advance of 50 Pounds enabled me to sail home to India – and my long literary journey as a freelance writer.

We did not have many books published in India in the 1950s and '60s, so most of my work was published in newspapers and magazines, and my income from these sources just about kept me afloat. I had been living in Delhi for several years, but city life did not inspire me, and in 1963 I moved to the hill-station of Mussoorie.

Here I found a cottage in the woods, and the stories began to flow like the wind from the mountain passes.

Stories such as *The Blue Umbrella*, *Angry River*, *The Room of Many Colours* and *Cherry Tree* were published here and in other countries, and helped to establish me as a children's writer. And early stories, such as *Night Train at Deoli* and *Time Stops at Shamli* were being reprinted.

Publishers were springing up everywhere. And so were my books!

Seventy years after starting out, I'm still writing - and enjoying every moment of it.

It's all an adventure –
setting out to do what you
want to do, then doing it,
struggling against the
tide, managing the ups
and downs, highs and
lows, of the life you
have chosen.
It's never smooth
sailing.

An adventure is never without risk. But the ultimate reward is greater than the risk.

You will have the satisfaction of having achieved something worthwhile, given meaning to your life, inspired others, done something different, left your mark upon the planet!

As a writer, what have I achieved, apart from my own personal happiness? I have led children by the hand, or rather by the written word, to a love of books, of language, of creative activity. Books give pleasure, but they also help you to think for yourself.

Look upon life
as an adventure
- an adventure in
which you have
set your heart on
reaching the top
of a mountain -
a mountain of
your choice.

The climb to the top is never easy, but once you are there, you will find that there is nothing to equal the sensation...

of being on top of the world.

And you can go further and reach for the stars!

**Ruskin Bond**

# Paddle Your Own Canoe

There's a little proverb that I remember from my childhood. My father even inscribed it in my autograph album.

Row your own boat, don't depend on someone else...

...who may or may not be a good rower and who won't know where to take you.

Be familiar with your canoe or your bike or your car,

and
paddle
or peddle
or drive it
yourself.

You know
best
where you
want to go,
what you
want to do
in life.

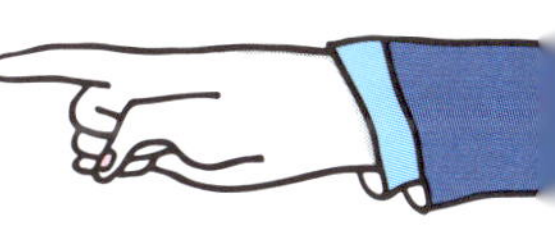

Don't let others shake your resolve. Don't let stormy waters halt your progress.

There's something you want at the end of your little journey, and the best way of getting it is through your own skills.

Paddle away!

Sometimes, when there is a road block, you take a side-street or little-used lane to reach your destination.

In the journey of life,
we will come
across many
road-blocks,
most of them
devised by
fellow humans.
To avoid them,
we must learn
to zig-zag, look for
alternate routes.

Don't be
discouraged.
There's always
another road,
another means
of getting where
you want to go.

# REmEmbER...

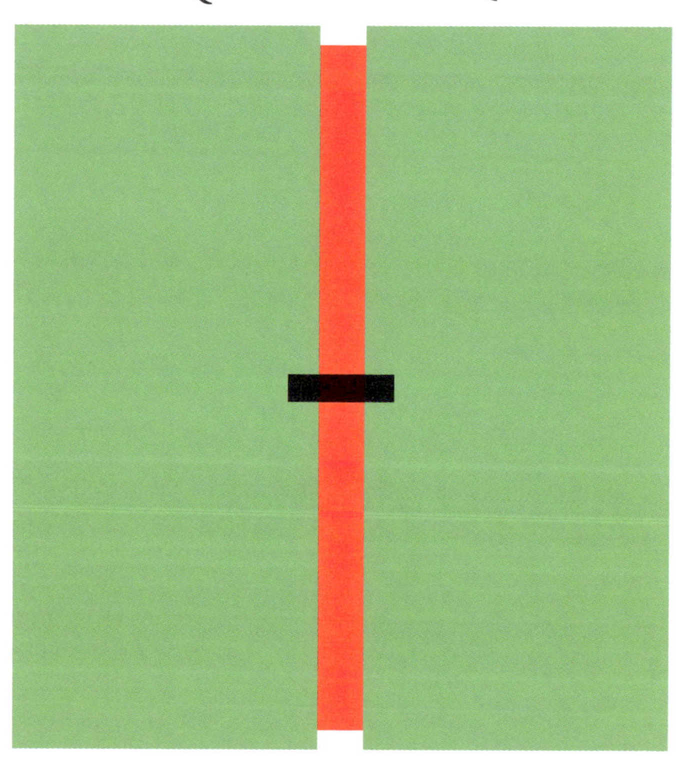

WHEn onE dOOR clOSES,

Another

door opens.

If a particular line of work, or study, or occupation doesn't suit you, look for another. Zig-zag until you find it. If you don't like your job, look for another.

If you don't like the town or environment in which you live, go in search of another. Don't feel chained to one place, one situation.

Zig-zagging

also gives you a fresh

and different view

of the world around you.

Not only will you see

more of the world,

but the world

will see more of

you!

# Be Greedy

I don't mean being greedy for your little sister's share of the cake, grabbing it from her and gobbling it.

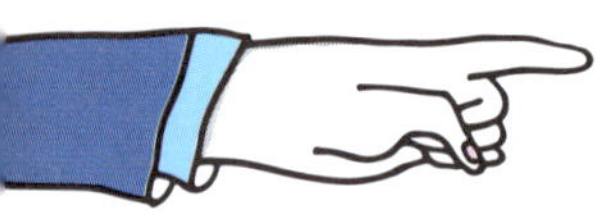

Be greedy for
the good things
of life, for
life itself and
all that it has
to offer.

I'm ninety years old, but am I satisfied? Not quite. Much as I'm grateful for the ninety years I've spent on this amazing planet, I'd love to have a little more of it – flowers in bloom, kingfishers in flight, crickets singing, bumble-bees buzzing, gazelles leaping, cattle grazing, mountain streams murmuring, stars twinkling, moonbeams spreading, the dawn breaking.

When we are nine
we take all this
for granted.

When we are
ninety we want
more of it.

# Be greedy for life, most precious of gifts.

Don't just
take it for
granted.

# Practice Makes Perfect

If you want to be a tennis champion, you must practise – and keep practising!

If you want to excel at cricket, you'll have to practise hitting those sixes. Or if you want to be a great bowler like Bumrah, you'll practise your art between matches, you won't take success for granted.

If you're a chess player, you'll practise.

If you are an archer, you'll practise.

If you're an athlete, you won't stop running.

I'm not an athlete, so I don't run except when there's an angry bear just behind me.

Being a writer,
I practise
putting words
and sentences
together in an
interesting way.

The great musicians are always practising, whether they play the sitar or the violin or the saxophone.

If a great singer doesn't practise regularly, he'll miss a note at a crucial moment!

Don't try to be a singer or musician unless you are really good at it. And then, practise.

Know what you
are good at, and
if it's what you
want to do, do it
well. Don't stop
practising!

# Knowledge Is Power

That doesn't sound very exciting, but it's true.

The more we **know,** the further

we can gó!

The lessons you have to learn in your
school curriculum aren't enough. You must
explore the subjects that interest you. Brush
up your history. Read about the rest of the
world and how it lives. Not just the United
States, where everyone wants to go. There
are fascinating lands waiting for you to
discover them – Madagascar, Fiji, the West
Indies, Peru, Finland, Japan, Borneo…

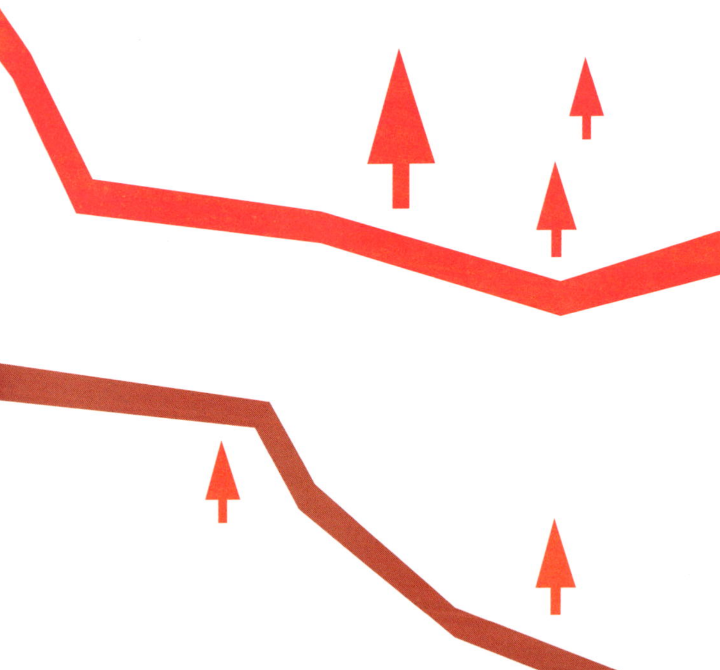

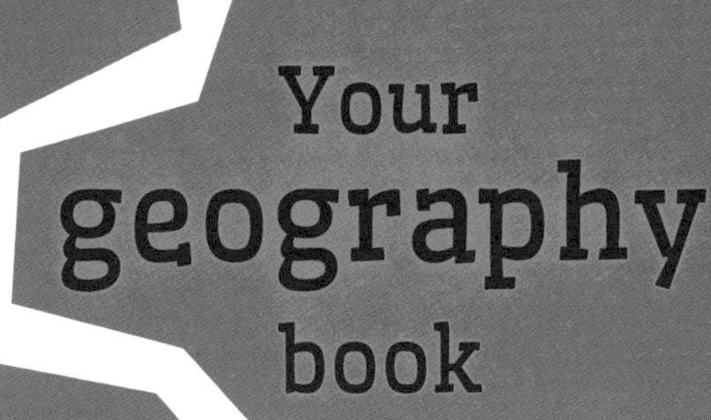

Your
geography
book
will only give you
a few facts
about
other lands.
You must
discover them
yourself.

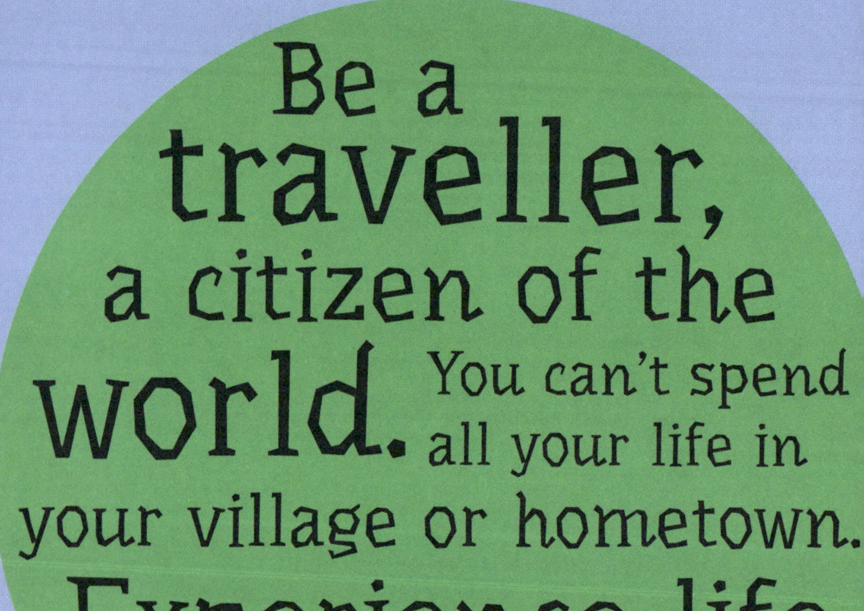

Be a traveller, a citizen of the world. You can't spend all your life in your village or hometown. Experience life to the full. You can always come home again.

# Courage

Your life is shaped by the courage you bring to it. Be bold! If you want to reach the top of your profession, your vocation, cast aside timidity.

If you have ideas,
make them known.
If you have a gift,
     put it to good use.
If you can act,
     be an          actor.
If you can          write,
be an author.
     If you can     sing,
don't stop singing!

If you are good at
business,
be an entrepreneur.
If you like the sea,
join the navy.
If you like to fly,
be a pilot – or
an air-hostess!

But if you're lazy and like to be in bed all day, you might well end up making other people's beds for a living.

# Get Out Of Bed

**Beds** are wonderful inventions, designed to rest the human body after a hard day's work.

But for some, they are designed for rest after a night of partying hard. Parties can be fun, and life would be dull without them, but the habit of lying in bed till noon is an indulgence that leads to a lack of ambition and a reluctance to get going in the race for whatever we want to achieve.

You don't have to be up with the lark or your neighbour's poultry, you don't have to join the joggers and fitness freaks in the park. But you might at least welcome the rising sun, for it's the sun that keeps you and your fellow beings alive, as residents of Planet Earth.

Don't take this for granted. Make Get up with the little sunshine always be bedtime.

world, this life
the most of it.
sun and spread a
yourself. It can't

# The Come-Back Kids

Sometimes the most successful among us find our winning ways are crushed for a time – by accident, injury, illness or some stroke of misfortune.

If we have the will and resilience to recover from a setback, there will be no stopping us on our way to personal glory.

Not so long ago, the gifted cricketer Rishabh Pant was involved in a horrific road accident. His car caught fire and he suffered serious burns and other injuries which kept him in hospital for months. But as soon as he was better he was out on the field, exercising and practising his batting and wicket-keeping skills. Before long he was captaining the Delhi Capitals IPL team, scoring runs and taking wickets. And then he was back on the World Cup T20 team, heading for the West Indies. There was no stopping him!

I can think of the great sportsmen who have made comebacks after periods of defeat or physical setbacks: the golfer Tiger Woods; the great heavyweight boxing champion Mohammed Ali; the football genius Maradona; the racing-car driver Lewis

Hamilton among many others...

There have been several women achievers too who overcame all odds to excel in their chosen fields – Serena Williams who faced health issues and injuries throughout her career and yet came out on top to win multiple Grand Slam titles; Bethany Hamilton, the professional surfer who lost her left arm in a shark attack and returned to competitive sailing a year later. Closer home, Mary Kom who defied all odds to become the first Indian boxer to win a medal at the Olympics and Arunima Sinha who climbed Mount Everest after losing a leg in a train accident making her the first PWD woman to achieve such a feat, to name just a few.

Some struggled with injury, some with

drugs, some with depression... But they overcame despair and reached the heights again.

Never despair. But if you do, then work in despair. Your skills and your determination will help you to prevail.

NO

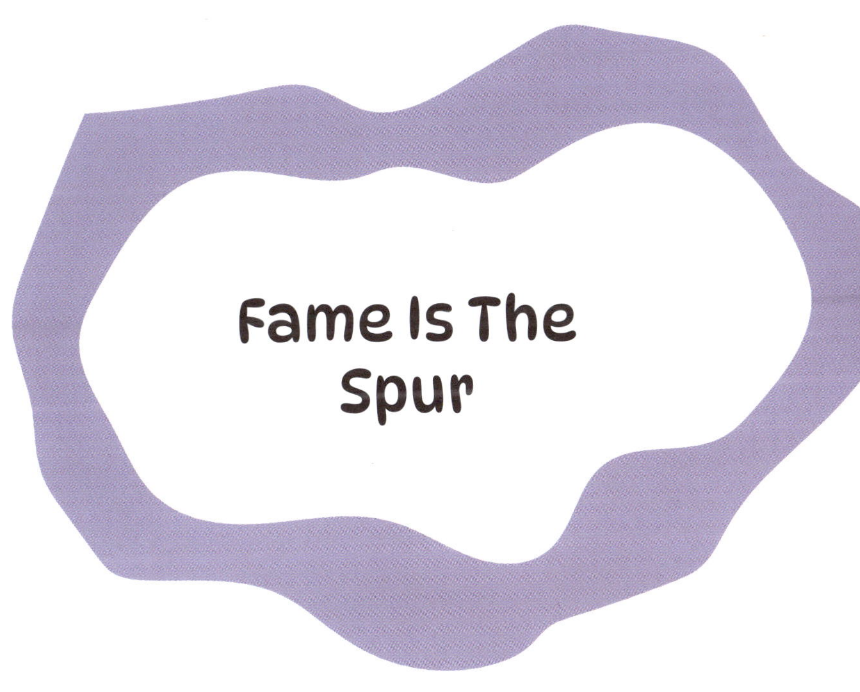

# Fame Is The Spur

The desire for fame and fortune has often been the driving force behind the successful lives of film stars, sportsmen, pop singers and others who make the headlines.

It takes **hard work** and **ambition** to reach the status of a celebrity, especially in the entertainment world.

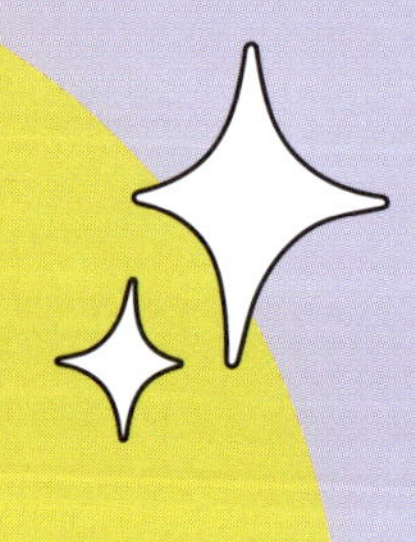

But there's a price to pay for this kind of fame: the loss of privacy; the constant attention of fans and media; the pressure to stay at the top, for it's so easy to fall from grace, to take a wrong step and slip off the ladder of success. It may not be worth all the tension, pressure and rivalry that you will have to go through.

**You need a calm temperament in order to deal with fame and all the stress that it brings. Don't let it get to you. Stay calm.**

Be respectful
to those you
work with. Don't
show off. Help
those who are
struggling to
make a mark.

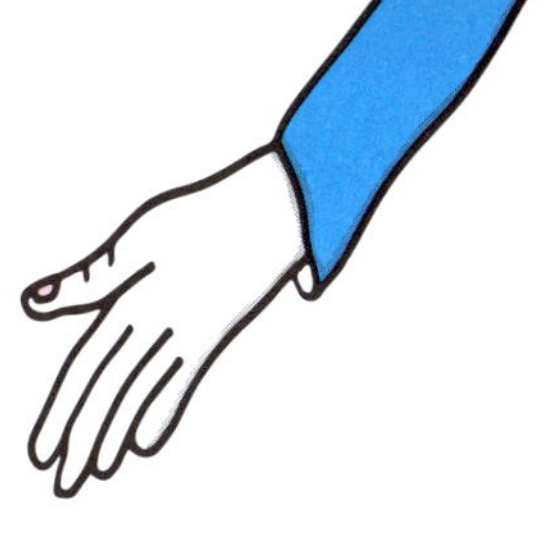

**Above all, you must continue to enjoy doing what made you famous – whether it's singing or acting, kicking a football, chasing a cricket ball (fielding should be as much fun as hitting sixes!), throwing a javelin, or running the marathon.**

And if, like me, you come last in the marathon, it's better to try something else. Stick to what you are good at!

ALL GLORY
COMES FROM
DARING TO
BEGIN.

DON'T LEAVE YOUR BEST EFFORT UNTIL IT'S TOO LATE. THERE ARE TWELVE HOURS IN A DAY, NOT THIRTEEN.

# Pull Your Own Strings

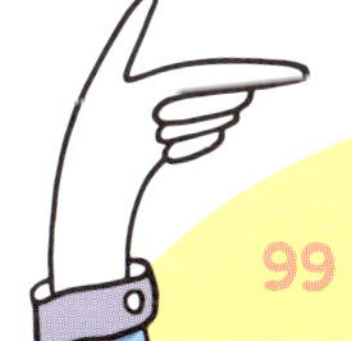

If you are a
strong-minded person,
you will want to do
something by yourself
— not depend on
Daddy's influence or
family connections or
all that money in the
bank.

You have to
put your own
talent on display
and not depend on
someone else's
success.

Learn to be independent. If it's a job you want, go out and look for it, don't wait for it to come to you.

When, at the age of 17, I arrived on the island of Jersey, in the U.K., I needed a job, any job, in order to survive. So I walked down the High Street in the little port town of St. Helier's, stopping at every office, shop, department store and offering my services as an assistant who could type, write a letter, do accounts or make the office tea.

Well, a travel agent took me on – to look after the office while she was enjoying the beach with her boyfriend! The job did not last long, but I soon found another, and it kept me going while I wrote my first book.

I was always ready to take on a job, and I found them for myself. And when I'd written my book, I went in search of a publisher without troubling someone for a foreword or introduction.

Self-reliance will get you through life more successfully than reliance on others. Take help when it's offered. Be grateful for it...

But don't depend on it.

In the long run, that man is strongest who stands alone.

# Some Don'ts

Please, **please**, keep away from **drugs**, the 'nasha' that only leads to **misery** and an...

untimely end.

I have seen too many promising young lives, wrecked by dependence on drugs, both soft and hard.

Don't go
swimming
among sharks.

(In other words, avoid the company of crooks, criminals and cheats–

the three 'c's of the underworld.)

Be kind to **animals,** but don't try curing a **tiger** off a **toothache.**

So go ahead...
Let nothing stop

# You

from being who

## You

want to

# Be!

Or from

being

YOU!

# About the author

**RUSKIN BOND** is one of India's most well-known writers. He was awarded the **Padma Shri** in 1999 and the **Padma Bhushan** in 2014. Ruskin Bond was selected for a **Sahitya Akademi Fellowship** in **2021**. His books with **HarperCollins** include, '**These Are A Few Of My Favourite Things**', '**Koki's Song**', '**How To Be A Writer**', '**How To Live Your Life**', '**How To Be Happy**', '**The Enchanted Cottage**', '**The Golden Years: The Many Joys Of Living A Good Long Life**' and '**Another Day In Landour**'. He lives in Landour, Mussoorie.

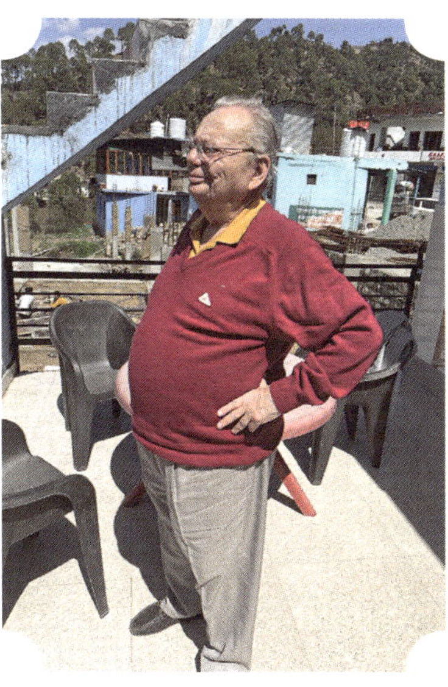

# About the illustrator and designer

**SHAMIKA CHAVES** is a children's book illustrator, author and graphic designer based in Mumbai, India. She successfully pursued a degree in applied art and has illustrated and designed over **25** children's books. She has worked with publishers including **HarperCollins Children's Books India**, **Scholastic India**, **Parragon Publishing India**, **Hachette India**, **Fingerprint Publishing India** among others. She lives and works in a cosy little home with her husband, Christopher.

Visit @shamikasdoodles on Instagram or www.shamikasdoodles.com to learn more about her work.

Flip the page to
see more in the
'How to...' series

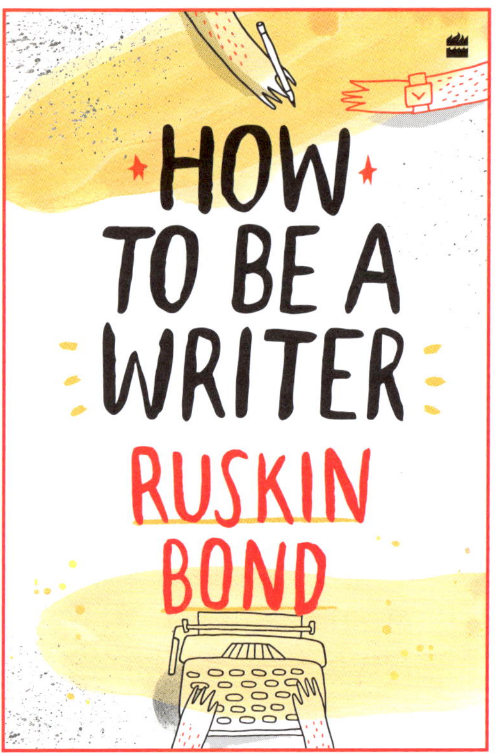


"Wherever I go, I meet young writers, or young people who want to write, and they are always asking questions.

Someone who has survived as a writer for over seventy-five years must have something to offer by way of 'tips' (as one young friend put it) or the lessons learnt from all the ups and downs of a literary journey."

**'How to be a Writer'** is peppered with nuggets of practical advice for every person who is aspiring to write and be published — all told in Ruskin Bond's characteristic understated, tongue-in-cheek, humorous style.

**This book is an exclusive glimpse into the writing credo of Ruskin Bond, an author who has had an incredibly successful writing career spanning over 75 years.**

'Fat' is an essential part of our systems, and we can't do without it. It is there in our food too. As I discovered when I opened my first book—*A Book of Nursery Rhymes*—and came across this rhyme:

> Jack Sprat
> could eat no fat,
> His wife
> could eat no lean,
> And so, between
> the two of them,
> They licked the
> platter clean.

A simple rhyme, but it does conjure up a picture of Mr. And Mrs. Sprat tucking into their supper.

Why do we associate being 'lean' or thin with a certain cunning and vindictiveness? We have Shakespeare to thank for that. "Yon Cassius has a lean and hungry look; he thinks too much: such men are dangerous." There you have the power of the pen. Are lean men dangerous? Of course not. But Cassius was, and we remember Cassius.

Fat boys are often described as being greedy. But sometimes being fat has nothing to do with food, it's a medical condition.

**Avoid stereotypes**

As writers, we should avoid creating stereotypes.

must start to develop your own style.

**Find your own style and voice**

For a young writer an easy, flowing style is best. Vary the length of your sentences, but don't let them get too long and involved. Study the style of one of the great masters of the short story, Somerset Maugham. He writes very simply, but he has the knack of getting to the heart and mind of his characters, of telling a story, and of carrying you along with him as the narrative progresses.

**Here are Maugham's strengths:**

- He has a good story to tell.
- His characters are real, interesting.
- He doesn't waste words.
- He is observant, he keeps a notebook.
- He has a recognisable style.

Apart from Maugham's novels and short

It's a letter, it's advice, it's a letter with advice, it's Ruskin Bond's definition of life...

"Be whatever you want to be... Give it your heart and soul, and you will have made something of your life, my friend, You are all my sons and daughters when it comes to telling you '**How to Live Your Life**'."

This is a book packed with all the good advice anyone, any age, would love and benefit from because it is sound wisdom distilled from the wonderful life and times of the inimitable Ruskin Bond, unmistakably one of India's most popular authors.

**Each piece of valuable advice is worth its weight in gold!**

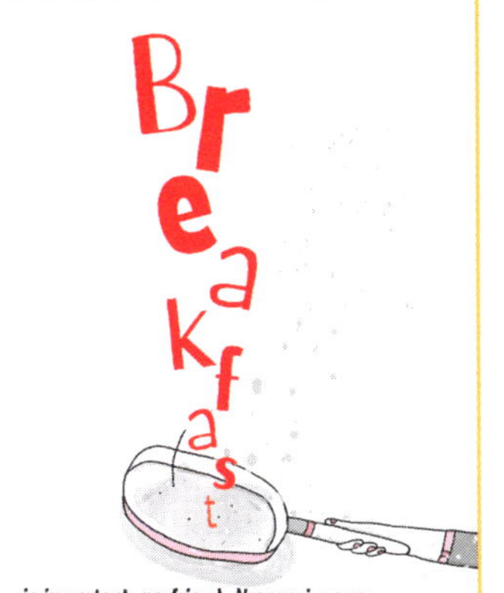


is important, my friend. Never miss your
breakfast. Food is important but what has
really sustained me all these years can be
summed up in one word:

WORDS

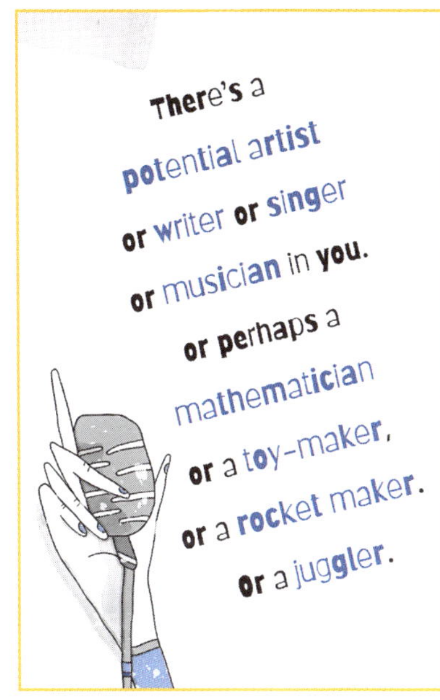

is the greatest healer.
And the human mind is adaptable.
The horrible days pass.
The lonely weeks pass.

Make
a friend.
Find friends.
Join a group of people
who are doing interesting things.
Some of the most balanced
people I know are
Bird
Watchers.

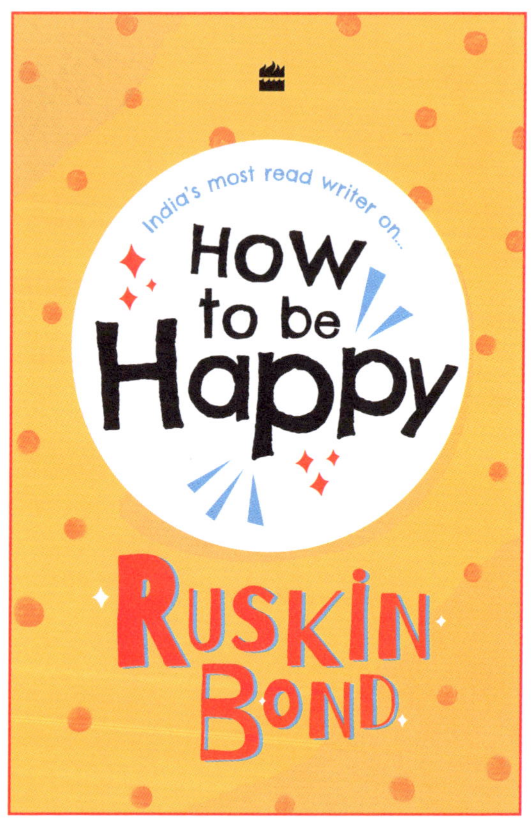


"You can't buy happiness. You can't get it wholesale or retail or online. It inhabits a small space in your mind, and you must look for it there."

This book carries decades of experience on how to be contented, how to lead a fulfilling life, how to inhabit the delightful world of books and stories, and most of all **how to be happy!**

Through the bright, happy pages of this book, Ruskin gives us advice that is sage, doable, relatable and most of all from the heart and the pen of a man who has lived a truly brilliant life.

Without that sun there would be no life on the planet. Greet it, salute it, for it signals a new day, a new beginning.

Let's justify our presence on this planet. And let's do it by trying to emulate the great creator. Create something, make something, even if it's only a clay pot. Remember, Christ in his youth was a carpenter, Krishna grazed the family's cows.

Busy hands will do something useful. And if guided by the mind they will create something we can cherish!